A Happening in Hades

Also by S. K. Kelen

Atomic Ballet
Dingo Sky
Trans-Sumatran Highway and other Poems
Dragon Rising
Shimmerings
Goddess of Mercy
Earthly Delights
Island Earth: New & Selected Poems
Yonder Blue Wild
Love's Philosophy: a Selection of Sonnet-like Creatures

A
Happening
in
Hades

S. K. Kelen

PUNCHER & WATTMANN

First published in 2020
Published by Puncher and Wattmann
PO Box 279
Waratah NSW 2298

http://www.puncherandwattmann.com
puncherandwattmann@bigpond.com

NATIONAL
LIBRARY
OF AUSTRALIA

A catalogue entry for this book is available from the National Library of Australia.

ISBN   9781925780611

Cover design by Miranda Douglas
Cover photo by S. K. Kelen

Printed by Lightning Source International

Contents

To the futures

Barbarian

Fey provincial folk played guitars
and zithers, slowly farmed the days
they read books and sat through plays
lived their lives creatively
(crochet, writing and pottery)
oblivious to the barbarian hordes
surrounding and then they noticed.
Hast thou forsaken me? each cried
to a private god. *Yo!* each god replied
Flood, famine, fire, advertisements,
the pitiless roar of distant engines.
Red lights, the home audience stare
at shiny screens. It is a Golden Age.
The barbarians watch and listen.

Parallel Worlds (Earth No. 47)

Sometimes slip into a parallel world,
then the one after that, it often happens flying.
It's a whole new universe when you land
and disembark. Sydney Airport Earth No. 47.
People speak slightly differently,
the airport's festooned with bright advertising
campaigns for brands and products that didn't exist
a week or so ago, football players you've never heard of
headline the national team. Everywhere a raw nervousness,
the talk gets giggly about a new war, the time to hate,
and who to hate, keep in mind the terrorist thrill,
sexy and mysterious. Join the fight to save Propaganda.
Make do in this tiger-free dimension—at least a while—
hotter here than the last world, things fall apart fast.

Parallel World Two (Earth No. 48)

And disembark. Sydney Airport Earth No. 48.
I grew blasé, details were different, but each world's
Fundamentals were pretty much the same, a stasis of constant flux:
Humans mistreating Nature (and hoping they could get away with it),
Love and entertainment, war and politics, eating, creating and destroying
So we can build, a race to top then the end we were too mesmerised
By reality stars' voluptuous flesh and eyes to see the forests die
And the oceans rise. Cataclysm made clear: from moment to moment
The universe changes. The change started when I flew in
From God-knows-where and God-knows-when.
The world suddenly tipped over into a new Age, something different.
It was the day after tomorrow the collapse began, the structures
Built and evolved over aeons faded and the striving died, replaced by
Grey resignation and regret that spans the globe. And life is quiet.

Golden Storms

Heed tales of heroes
who fell off the earth—
eaten by their dragons.
Time to keep faith
with common sense,
live happily and no longer be
dangerous, know Golden Storms
& other poems fulfil a function
save the world another day,
hope, perhaps, for your loves
alone. Empty the mind—
exalt the profound kitchen,
wash the dishes transcendence
transcend dance is enough

Eternity

Tetris plates, cups, saucers, spoons,
knives, forks, spatulas into a dishwasher
and st vitus dance a broom
(do this daily) sweep clean until doom
scrub and feel sun shine inside:
a servant of the house, sure,
but daydreaming afternoon
wrestle demons grown
in the garden. Just once the outside
world got in, at midday, there was
vicious cutlery, but storms brought quiet.
Today, a warrior made of plastic blocks
stands guard on the dining table, strong
vigil like a power ranger grandma.

Revenge: A Mystic's Guide

Friendly approach: Nature and Anger
provide and who you'd like to
take care of themselves. Be practical:
fire a flaming spirit-arrow,
point a bone, skin a live rat (dream karma)
do a cherry dance, hold a heart
in your hands. Use the telephone, a doll,
pins and needles, harness lightning
and the powers of television. Better still
remember to live well, powered by
Justice and serving enemies up cold.
Laughter and not hurting anybody,
a quiet sleep and the next day, peace.
Be kind when cruel, make it sweet.

Massachusetts Zombie Horror

Stay home forever to garden words, pale-inked
poems in a sober script and sprung rhythms. Black
carriages arrive at the stepping-off place over the road.
Evening in Fall, 1862, birds' sly cries, what is civilization?
A cold wind blows leaves like the names, unbearable to speak,
of boys shot & wasted. A brisk walk down Main Street
the wide world begins—hammer work, commerce,
sweat, adventure whisper (a visit to the general store),
town and country vista busy victualling the war.
Down the road, skeletons rattled like epigrams.
Foul corpse mouths swore oh it was worth it.
Gauche human error, ironies aboard
clipper ships, a plague of curses, and yet—
clever goodness, the future was electricity.

Hong Kong

Beneath the jet
clouds are white ceramic wisps
sky painted eggshell blue
Island Orient Pearl—
I love landing at your airport.

Disembark, breathe fresh diesel-scented
smog blown from Guangzhou
thick as turtle jelly a bitter tonic
taken since ancient times to toughen the lungs.
A shoebox apartment on the 88th floor
the cloud world lives in a shiny mall.
Nature entails fashion/Sexiness heralds health,
holiday pure islands intoxicate dancing
mango dessert courtesy 許留山 (Hui Lau Shan).

Soaring California

Anaheim's street dogs barked rock and
roll all night, a southern Californian party
succubus appeared in the bathroom mirror,
smiled, torched the en-suite, her flames
lit the motel room—fantasy-land firemen's flash flood
doused the fire, western-style. Flesh and spirit.
Ravening faux frippery kept proceedings slippery—
Doctor Sforzando woke from his prescription daze,
saw the future was robot and desert wind on a flat,
high-definition screen controlling people's lives.
Cold jetlag vision: hungry cars crawl the streets,
stalk haunted people hunting for their car keys.
Pay the succubus. Old Bacchus flies a Disney
rocket ride, belly laughs, his spirit thrives.

More Words: Uses for a Father

Swing pusher human monkey bars punching bag
stroller roller ball thrower toy finder magic trick
performer hide and seeker wrestler piggy back
bear/dog/monkey/elephant/cat/tiger/bird-pretender
trampoline story teller word teacher book reader
picture drawer food feeder drink dispenser librarian
taxi driver mess cleaner nappy changer bath maker
towel dryer sleep rocker garden guide song singer
fast bowler TV remote controller kite flier acrobat
safety net fierce warrior guard horsey ride—now
more words appear in my head pop out my mouth
make me laugh—bird bath apple pie big brother go
pick me up fight time cricket bat whack kick
box new fun. Time to play football. We run.

Ocean

Her stabbing stilettoes sweet
kisses in the sea-struck mind—
Love the hate the love-me,
love-me-nots hurt, so deep runs
the magic and sweet brutality
impossible to resist
the phone call to misery is
the fairy tale you live in, a story
unfolding by a cold river.
Insane now, so you feel this.
The meltdown. A toy slaps the mind.
Then the peace ray
beams down bliss and light
and miracles.

Sirens

Speed of light insomniac runs,
angry mantras burn the tongue,
falling masonry fire shock it's over.
Lifetime ago anger grew unbearable
a leader's words touched the spirit,
reading the texts elated: do this
for love and land, strike the heart,
avenge injustice. Old nightmare's fury
proved accurate driving there (no turning back)
smuggle the steel cylinders to the basement.
Flashlights beam the rubble. Remote-pilot
assassin birds visit villages, shower rockets.
Flashlights beam the rubble.
Cold winds blow from angry hearts.

Renovations

With the world about to end, oh, *begin*
its inexorable slide is less dramatic
after all, we'd been spoiled for weather—
though the disappearance of the polar ice
was dramatic in retrospect, but there was some
time left, enough, and around here people
just went extension- and renovation-mad,
our homes grew while the rivers dried
and the sky darkened with fumes
as if a new room with en-suite and walk-in
and a brick garage for the hybrid car
could hold back rising oceans, plus
a view beyond the neighbours and a freshly
paved barbecue area to honour coral reefs.

Happy Days

March winds blew summer away
today is a gorgeous autumn day.
What I see is great: a golden cockatoo
really a sulphur-crested cockatoo
ruffled white feathers haloed by the sun
this bird looked truly golden.
Crimson rosellas: flames flicker
on tree branches, wild budgerigars
yell their heads off & a suave lorikeet
says nothing, the gang-gang's call
cracks like a rifle shot sets the ducks and galahs
squawk and flapping. Quiet red gums shade
the cheery birds whistling, warbling a river day
the kids swim and play way back in 1993.

Dark Art

There were wars and hunger abroad,
misery, injustice and evil in the streets
but on the home front who could bear
a boredom deep as contentment thus Stupid
danced with Death at the pub, afterwards
in an ivy-tombed terrace house (built of gingerbread)
she opened a glamorous vial, just a whiff
put Stupid to sleep and she transplanted the dog's heart,
bit by bit into him, it hurt and for a while life
was lived in dirt—the world was desperate.
Voodoo puppet will live to regret (ironies befall).
The future. Cruel magic swarms happily
inside the leftover fun people. They blame a song
from youth for how old they got, or—not.

Sleep

Diluted by moonlight, industrial
strength sleep is not too deep
beyond what you imagine—
Ah to be in the crazed time and place
when music took us into space
and we saw flying saucers for real.
Before that it was rickety
metal and home rotting red bricks
the rockets to the moon, vitamins
and transistor radios designed by mad scientists—
sudden pharmacopeia, precision
machines, hallucinatory night-art-3D-music
an endless supply of paperbacks,
all were good reason
to shoot rockets into the heart.

Robot X

No lightning bolts from my fist
today, nor dramatic transformations
human to machine and back,
my zigzag ceased at midnight
I was a killer machine
confessing badness to the moon
when my brain seized
and the fighting stopped
I resumed a peaceful life
among animals and plants
but (no buts) robotic impulses
occasionally drive my actions
till the nervous system
reboots.

Drone

It was a metaphysical crisis only the
founding fathers' wisdom could contemplate
so President Z returned from the other side
transformed into the man some folks voted for
he was a great guy at a barbecue, or teeing off
he was like Honest Abe without a brain
whistling Dixie, axe to grind this time
it's personal the republic needs protecting
nothing will stop destiny, its termination
his soul was the ultimate sacrifice
take on whatever menace—
a lot of people will have to die
(undead presidents are rarely nice!)—
and save America, the world thereby—
exhausted.

Fish, Cat, Emu

Three tablets before meals:
Fukushima fish farm fresh fish oil
Caesium might fight diseases
and like the cat virus do funny
things to body and mind: (for instance)
grow whiskers and a tail!
Something keeps scratching
from inside—cat crystals
cut the mind, cranky sure,
too attached to computers I'll never
get over the silver wonder
whose motherboard failed and passed on.
Paint thick eyelashes round the emu's
big eyes she is a bird to behold!

Quotidian

True to type, rapt,
trapped by an embalming pipe
bling bling hums
the king bee's song,
hives grow honey life
compose a trance
then humans dance
barefoot on burning ice.
Seen it all, Tourist, now
some sanity in the house—

Commute

Motoring I wonder
does getting run over by a Nissan
hurt at all, hit by a Mercedes
blood spurts regally
a truck is workmanlike
when it crushes
black BMW leaves no evidence—
stormy thoughts
be thoughtless, happy, drive
home to a floating world.
Remember, the voices
in your head are just
thoughts talking.

Kiss

I missed kissing and caring more than a damn,
Missed her voice, her being next to me—
Wished to see her immediately and explain
How Marvell's poem 'To His Coy Mistress'
Was the preface to what I needed to say
To her, that we must grow flowers to celebrate
Time together and with joy, let Fate crazily delay
What's inevitable and nothing is hurt when we are together.
So I composed an old fashioned ode, transmitted
To her on the astral plane via the magic of electricity.
I wrote words like love and passion, used imagery.
I came to life when we kissed, flying on a picnic blanket
To the lawns at the gardens of Versailles Palace
Lush as her eyes when she smiled and I counted the ways.

Populist Mongering

Said is done all done and said (?) in thrall
a self's daily selfies' words hammered to contort
nowhere and peter out an unfinished thought
imply a voice on its own was clever crafting cliché
into something else itself all meaning no more (please), each day
We witnessed miracle the endless waltz with self—
self discovery gave birth to itself, a family of moments
in portrait mode, the disgust for the world gifted us
pure and passive as self-pity, raged, elated and plucked
on waxed wings soared to the heights self regard permitted
It was sincere, and unselfish: a self polished to save
the world and the self-generation responded with praise epic
one of us could be the babiest diddums of them all and the bird
in the bush descended slowly, branch to flower to stick

Ongtupqa (Grand Canyon)

Soft talk on the tour bus, camera glow
and flash, nodding off during day-dream video:
mule trains edge the narrow paths back in silent
black and white times. The driver/guide
kept up the commentary. The Hoover Dam flew by.
Quorum of squirrels and lizards watch the tourists
step off the bus, shade eyes chilled by sunlight
and look down the beautiful crack in the Earth
a mile deep, a taste of sweet boulders and vertigo.
When a crow soars see through the crow's eyes.
Cactus, brush, stone frame yellow, red sand.
A black hawk elevates. The escape across thin air
ellipsis lasts a metre then down you fall, the signs
warned, the story goes, an artist capturing the view.
A lonely cloud whispers get on the bus back to Vegas.

The Nothing Days

Thursday (what date is it?
Begin forgetting), Nothing Thursday
Nothing Friday Nothing Saturday Sunday
Monday. Recite Nothing each day.
Practise this Tuesday and Thursdays
Days easily confused, they run widdershins
Last week vanished up a tree.
Or say Wednesday (note: remember: read to-do list)
Concentrate on breathing all day. Say nothing,
The day is full of hours
Breaking down to minutes, seconds
All the way to never. Stop. Think, say nothing.
Nothing every day, today. Forgotten.
Say anything and there will be trouble.

Paris

Am an archive knee deep in autumn.
Raking time, leaves keep falling.
Rescued one of eternity's foundlings:
Who reads a hundred poems
writes like a hundred poets;
who reads a thousand poems
writes like himself.
was how it goes—approximately!
Ancient Chinese proverb
(anonymous), autumn
time think hot, cold eternities.
Days, weeks, falling leaves.

Empire of the Scene

The bitchfest of contemporary continues
well into the new. Vases of runcible flowers
are placed on shelves memorialising dust to dust,
the ceremony dates back thousands of years.
Who's in? Who's out? Depressed by the emperor's lust
for mahogany shades? Were the glaring omissions intentional?
Literary flavours tasted, favours are re-visited, grudges settled,
beer clout sketched; editors' friendships celebrated.
Luckily there's a love interest. Lavinia, the pneumatic,
bookish polymath's finger-wagging verse gained a more
than generous berth on the shelf. Imagine keyboards rattlin'
tender letters 'twixt soul-mates girdling virtual Earth.
The wooden flowers thrum so consider these wavy Etruscan
sonnets, grant them space in the anthology of doubt.

The Great Australian Noun

Thanks for the ding in the car's left front
panel, and the long key gash across the duco
some ____ left as a calling card, the final straw
for a ____ of a day when everything that can
go wrong does then the ____ over the road
plays awful music loud all night. Australians say
the blanked-out word with stupid youth's relish
and abandon, yelling at his mates skylarking
jump in and out a service station's automatic doors,
'you silly ____' but at night blessed souls
recall the noun's holy origin and why it should
only be whispered. Too crude for psychological
decryption: so many who cannot see the affront
make profane the sacred—that's enough.

Home Torture

X-Ray's invisible interrogator
steps out of a twisted back
punishes the slightest movement.
Pain plays the spine like a xylophone
hipbone pulls the torn left lower back
muscle, one false move and vertebrae
might pop out so the body must turn slowly
until the muscle-tearing stops
each leg finds a less painful angle
feet find footing so the back
avoids coming apart the legs push up
like a crab levitating—and pain plays
spooky circus music up the spine,
get out of bed, walk to the refrigerator.

Floating World

Pompoususs wrote to say how better
Than anyone else's his verse was,
Spent too many words about it, and ah
The world did not yet love him
Quite enough. So full of laziness and crazy
With the world's voices, endless leaves
Piling in the roof gutters, how to reply?
I determined not to write that letter,
Not one letter. The years flew.
Fearless sprinted across a field, mad
Muscles whispered, crows and magpies,
Sundry brown and mottled birds
Paid attention, oh why is everything blue
Today, not bright, the sky dark and sad
A day for never writing letters.

Online

It's good to google and find the truth,
a cure, friend, conspiracy, prophecies
for better and worse, more light hearted
robot erotica lightens the mood
as you trawl the world for a companion—
naked as Skype and the fish in the sea—
crazy in love online, video/upload
real life, heart processor sings 'ain't nothing
like a dame.' Meet in a photo at the airport,
your wikileak cheat-sheet sweetheart, virtual
tears, face-book her; love is twittering *who cares*
the daily beast, information baby, like
a burning *Sydney Morning Herald*. Photos.
Home page. Messages. A happy house.

Packing Up the House

Dreams are powerful, can bring the once living
back to life. The other night I was at the old family home
helping my parents pack up the house.
Working solidly while Mum kept us refreshed
with iced lime cordial. Still working in the early morning
I asked, *Why are we packing where are you going?*
Mum said, *You'll know soon enough, we have to go,*
get cracking we don't have forever. I was confused
not prepared for any of this then Dad was here,
so much younger than when I last saw him. Athletic,
in fine spirit, Dad rested his hand on my shoulder,
laughed and whispered, *actually it's all about forever*
don't be sad, your mother and I are already there.
Just bring your kids up right and take good care.

A Courtesan's Complaint

Shaking hands
I know only clouds.

Venice and Lido

1.

A wooden speed boat roars,
a gondola jumps in its wake.
Waves menace the quays
flood public squares
but the ocean lets Venice live
because its buildings
are so beautiful, painted bold pastels
pink, green, brown, red and blue
(coral colours the ocean likes)
and kept tidy over centuries—
Venice is the ocean's pet.
The canals are kept clean and the sea
mentioned with quiet respect,
save the slogan on a punk t-shirt:
See Venice Before It Sinks
The dredgers and pumps work all day.
Venice floats.
Pigeons at San Marco don't care,
tripping up tourists distracted by
a clever cornice, or a gargoyle griffin
its look of terror, and
how the sun's movement across the sky
changes tones and shades,
blue morning, vermillion evening.
The tourist crush pushes through alleys
into piazzas, marching in squares,
noticing a sea-borne basilica
some say, *wow look.*
The tourists bump into each other,
stunned by the Past's fine use

of colour, proportion and perspective,
the Golden Ratio works everywhere, say,
seventy percent of the human body is water
thus affinity with cloud, rain, canal.
A day on the ferry, a cold squall
listening to Italian spoken all the time
is like being at an opera of talking,
a grand music of vowels.

2.

Lido's dilapidated grand hotels
still serve huge breakfasts praised in nineteenth
century guidebooks, with quotes from Garibaldi's
cohort who, like all famished revolutionaries,
needed a hearty start to the day.
Many new camera species first appear
on Lido's streets, zoom and click a photo.
Complete strangers, and luxurious
gelati are grown, a heavenly lick's
exchange rate: one scoop per euro.
Here, everyone speaks *Football*
Angry words are rarely spoken.
People come to visit the islands of Venice to be alone
with a special other, surrounded by ocean.
Buonasera, nod to fellow travellers
a shared sense of respecting the punctilios
retiring to the shabby pensione's discreet,
scrubbed rooms. On the beach
a thousand changing sheds and deck chairs
stand to attention. They are alone in Winter.
Lido is a continent, to be remembered
in the deep future, like Atlantis.

Chiang Mai

Night Zoo Safari
giraffe purple tongue
saliva licks.

Noodle-fed dragons
and happy buddhas
hold up the sky.

The temple roofs
are rockets launching,
the houses float.

Traffic kicks along
(a firm Thai massage)
hot but not too humid,

air cleaner than Bangkok
the southern nightlife arrived
red-light bars and the boys, girls

and ladyboys line up in the streets.
There are trees in the city and
on top of the mountain, Doi Suthep,

the remains of mighty forest surrounding
the wat with famous views, gibbons' ghosts
swing from branch to branch

(they used to live here),
there's a poem or aphorism
pinned to every tree.

Wild forests are for the distance
or the long gone. The minibus will
take you back to town in time for the night

markets near the river, you will embrace
amorphous ambiguity, smile no,
say Zero times nothing equals, so

cling tight to your certainties,
and beware the market salad.
There is more water in the air

now than there used to be
say, thirty years ago, more
soft spots in reality.

Amsterdam Free City Epode

As is common in the west, there is no cuisine,
just the local food, supermarket and Asian.

People smoke and they toke and joke a lot they'll
crack on if they can in a coffee shop

Amsterdam Free City. Magic city smoking makes
people healthy. Grey clouds hang lazily

above the green canals. The tourists are over the moon
sip international beer eat a fabulous breakfast

and inhale burnt fruit of the Flower Academy
talk endlessly ideas exciting

travel tales, tall or true Burma to El Salvador
Eternity and beyond,

the Mamasan fresh fruit juices keep the dealers
healthy as they chop

and weigh the hashish, alert as cowboys, smart and alien
as the juicy girls in the brothels' windows

performing shameless gymnastics, all tits and crutch and arse,
for all the world to see—sex is on the map—

watching the girls leaves a taste like Dutch ambrosia cheese,
Friesian cows grazed on a stolen sea bed.

Sea wind blows fresh in Amsterdam and for the moment
the ocean is tricked by the canals.

Some places are meant to be under water and the city
was built with Atlantis in mind:

it rains and rains. The trams meander to suburbs whose names
sound like Led Zeppelin and Wettering Shunt.

The locals are cheerful and eager to give directions
the nearest bar or coffee shop full of smoke

and raving *kiff*-eating folk might say, 'get thee to a croissanterie.'
Always cool or cold here, the sky is mostly film noir grey

rain all the time. The dizzy sleep upstairs in narrow terrace houses—
a steep stairwell you can fall down in the morning.

Teetotal

Home, home, home,
That's the song of them that roam,
The song of the roaring, rolling sea
Is all about rolling home.
Bill Barnacle, 'Salt Junk Sarah'

Friday night, rolling home,
Wednesday, and lunchtimes, too, rolling
back to work, months and years,
and there's a glass or two at home.

Spirits fire up the spirit, gin for the body
whiskey instigates great works in the mind
that might continue for days,
mad, bad times, luxury Bacchus
raving in the pub feel the world spin, physical.
Beer chaser for the vitamins—
drank wild turkey like water
happy with everything

a drink or two or three and more
(the devil's claw), did the trick
and the years rotted high on the mast
then one night Stop says not another drop.
An instinct fizzles out... lost genre, a river of beer
trickles into the sand. The deepest divorce—
a drinker with his grog.

Nobody trusts an abstainer, turned
on his best friend drink, the poor sap
sips lemonade and new mates
at the Wowser Hotel submerse his soul

under a yard of common sense.
Time runs like water from the tap
clarity's less twisted (in the morning no
stranger calls you back to bed) o happy head,
the days are fresh. Suburb breathes sunshine oxygen,
the avenues: quiet, dappled, spiritual.

Approaching the Gnomic

Canine

a dog likes to roll
among dead animal pelt
smell like a hero

Ceremony

complex cure for sex
addiction—lovers grow up
behave with reason

The End

when the siecle
goes fin-fin that's the final
fin de siecle

The Gods

Zeus' Peanut Butter
Olympian crunchy taste:
no nut left to waste

Late Afternoon

afternoon storm clouds
cast shadow on village green—
Lightning bats, Thunder bowls

Jetsons

stronger than steel or
battery we outlive machines
the greedy gods drive

People's Republic

you used to be a
bony wreck now you're fat, cashed
up, and oozing sex

Good Stuff

stuff will rot the guts
kill the brain it transports one
to a higher plane

Ex Machina

Words the dead said
embodied the thoughts they had,
some written down on paper

mailed to and read by another dead
person, but while they were alive,
living their Age, having their time

and these words can stay with us
the famous saying
a catchy line, timeless

signifying a time, an era,
a flash, of History—
though most that's said

just disappears—
words just blurted out
gone nowhere,

slipped into the aether,
Space or wherever
words go when they go,

some very beautiful words
got lost in time and space
great-grandparents' words

gossamer and lace
floating above a bright atoll
mist in a churchyard

or settling over a plateau
grinding wars and sunny holidays
hand-written on curled postcards.

Goodbyes and hellos
(hey, missing you...)
words meant never said,

their sweet oblivion
silent, therefore of great
power and music,

words we didn't listen to
when we had the chance
should have read more closely

things best left unsaid,
the way angry words live many lives
come back and haunt us,

a note nailed to your heart
flutters at night
with the planets and stars

breathless, sad, remembering—
etheric words orbit an orb,
hang around,

need a pen, keyboard,
a terminal
or lips transfixed

will give body to lost speech,
crumbling type font
newsprint and dusty old books

maps, journals, children's first words
scribbled on the back of a photo
ancient magazines, talking heads

on black & white TV, crackling radio talk
broadcast a century ago.
The undeparted utterances—

every word is touchable
until it begins to fade.
Conversations

dangle on the other side—
the walls between are paper-thin,
an email arrives, full of whispering.

Dog Day

1.

He's grey muzzled now, the old kelpie
was always like a sun bear.
He lags and dawdles, smells the flowers,
grass & dog scents. Deaf or pretending
he doesn't catch up till he feels like
or the scent-spell breaks trots and slows
again, nearing home I stop and pat his head
remind him of the rules of going for a walk—
dogs walk not too far ahead psychically explain why
via Zeno's Paradox the sprinter Achilles
can never catch the tortoise nor an arrow reach the target
because infinite regression stops time
each step contains a puzzle of steps
that logic cannot overcome: you're fine until half-way
the remaining half splits in half and a step splits in half
that splits in half ad infinitum
there's no finishing, no destinations,
not a step completes: a thrown stick frozen in mid-air.

2.

Benjie's ears twitch and eyes gleam.
Next morning the paradox takes hold
he stops still as if doubting movement's possibility,
a tentative paw, sniffs a scent and runs free, dog logic
liberates so we step in the same river.

3.

Once upon a time there had been young kids
to chase him all afternoon but they grew up
and he stayed with Dad. The backyard
was a boneyard, dog bones—you mean cow bones
the butcher said this morning—o so many bones
it's not so bad not escaping dig the bone bury it in another spot
criss-crossing the yard transferring the meaty ones
chewed red, filthy with dirt, then with his claws
delicately digging a hole so when the bone's buried
not a grass blade or a rock is out of place,
old master dog at work.

4.

When he was young he was
the speed-of-light ball-fetcher
outran the Frisbee—fastest dog
this side of a whippet his rugby moves
evaded every kid on the oval. Escape artist
par excellence if he got ahead on a walk
or at home, the front door left open
a blink of the eye he'd bolted.
He'd wandered as far as Queanbeyan
hung out in Civic, the cheerful
nightclub patrons gave him hot dogs,
a couple of turns at the city pound...
Today I found him sleeping in the sun,
gone for a long walk. Ah, Benjie.

Playground Devils

The Diarist

Inside, the head
does its own work
builds psycho dreams
blows it all up a journal
kept of who I'd like to kill
—among other things—
the nerds who study and do well
those conceited athletes
one by one—the stupid headmaster
slobbering the microphone,
a lost tongue in his mouth
escaped from its dog owner—
and the teachers all lining up
a gaggle of tortured geese (metaphor)
praising high achieving dickheads
always trying their best, doing well,
well not everyone's well and they all, they all will…
An aeroplane flies over, shoot it down.
Hate reading books and never do it any more
because they rarely entertain as much as giggling
at my own thoughts or thinking about what my friends
are probably getting up to. Some of that teen fiction
we did in Year 8 was okay though—'specially
The Outsiders with Ponyboy and Soda Pop
by what's her name the author.
It made you feel really cool to be a rebel
if I learned one thing from books
it is a hero chooses to be 'dysfunctional'
as the counsellors call it.
Guess I hated the teachers most of all

gave 'em hell they couldn't stand me.
Failing the finals was gratifying
one of life's rare quiet moments.
The next act involves smashing
and crashing, no plan or golden path
to stray from getting bashed & bashing.
Days and nights of no respect whatsoever
angry, smash and smash. Let me loose
in the nearest village, you'll learn
about burn & pillage. Next year,
I'll be back, back on track.

Coach Idiot

falls for the ditzy teenager's goo-goo eyes
the crush works its way to find the fool
who lives in a foolish heart (o rose thou art sick)
& stupidity's blow-up rubber shark is about
to tear his life apart, a mind that can't control
the tool: whatever he's got he'll bet the lot

won't shy on taking a shot in the dark a champion fool
when his balls take the helm his brain won't save him
so far gone has he gone he'll think it's worth dying
the goo-goo eyes, now the deed's done voodoo
will come a lycra tracksuit's no shield against the talk
that gets you caught, forget ever working again,

at least in this town. Education got too physical,
the way out is no cool path. Going down—
at least the devil had wings to slow his descent,
fools don't—fools just fall. A statement
is read at morning tea in the common room—
a few coughs, a quiet curse muttered.

The Hoozees

From behind smack to the side of the head, turn
around, it's the youngest Hoozee he couldn't hurt a fly,
but his four brothers are there, too, pestering the girls
hitting the younger kids in the head, after all it's a
school social. Instead of minding your business
you tell them to piss off so they're all on to you,
grabbing and taunting with punches trying to get
a hold, the other brothers are arriving, cousins too
and mates a platoon of them getting stuck in
it's okay at first (kick box classes paying off)
don't feel the punches thanks to the adrenalin
you knock down one, two, floored the third
but still they're coming running in, it's worse
when they hold you back and the solid one
who can really fight lays in with hard punches unblocked
and pulps your head. Four more Hoozees arrive
and put the boot in, you're a bloody, broken mess—
but you'll survive. In a way you were lucky 'cos
backing them all up is big bro' Simo who last year
knocked out the head of the _____ Motorcycle gang
who'd gone round to see who this smartarse
Simo thought he was with his reputation
& with just one punch Simo left the bastard
flat out cold on the Hoozee welcome mat.
If he'd turned up you'd have been cactus.

Layabout

It's hard getting up before lunchtime
when the bed is as warm as the womb,
outdoors the morning is a sunlit tomb
that would burn and turn me to dust
a futile break in time and space
when daytime people are awake.
Dragging what's left out of bed
to a comfortable lounge no psycho
on an ego trip, no bastard's
going to tell me what to do
or be on time.
A job prospect rears its ugly head
but I got lost on the way to the interview.
Sleeping all day makes it easy to
stay up all night and the mates egg on
the brain bubbles and evaporates.
Spoilt? I've been hard done by...
Like a nagging caseworker, the dole
form reminds me I can read and write.
A beast, inanition, lurks at the back
of the brain, most people release it
on holidays and weekends
but when it takes over
there's not a spark, not two flint
stones struck together,
it made me a beastly child
and the beast grew in me, so
I'm just living on the planet,
absorbing what's said on television,
on the internet. What are you?
(We're all dust, anyway.)
Don't care at all, but believing,

still believing everything I want to,
and be cruel to those who love me,
fall into a Snow White sleep,
(ah! slow, tragic and deep,
a kiss of pity!) perfecting the art
of breaking a loved one or two's heart,
Mother, Father, or you, baby
it's hard to choose—or maybe all three
and any more that come to mind—
until cool sleep calls.

Bush Town

The town's idle few wrote poems that all sounded the same
Galloped and rhythmed and rhymed, writing was a game
Making words, however un-relevant, rhyme.
Rhyme they must, incessantly, always, all the time.
That narration must impart routine was rule nine—
The stories behind them were inevitably bad,
An anecdote about a pair of shoes and a cow gone mad
Teased out to fifteen pages and the reciting took ages
Is fair evidence of the town's galloping plight
(Verse once so strictly equestrian had become bovine)
The rhymes were forced, tortured, lame, sad
To have been created at all, destined for the knackery
And a square of light flickered menace, cast by the flame
Of remembrance and breathing smoke was an evil magician,
District Writers Committee Treasurer and Chairperson,
Tutor and Taste Arbiter, an Adam Lindsay Gordon acolyte
And a devil in his spare time, cast a gin and tonic spell,
Invoked the magic of creative writing quackery
With a sing-song soundtrack—the stock riders lined up
To workshop limericks squeezing yet another rhyme
With a dash of lemon and a dash of, sneaking in an extra line
That rhymed with rhyme. Patriotically, the bush town
Poets beat the favourite and won the cup—this time.

Discursive

The Contretemps are at it
making a point and sticking to it.
they yell and frighten the kids
who, liking anger learn to argue
and growing up, will be of two minds,
neither pleasant but there are issues to be raised,
disputes to resolve. Property, like young children,
must eventually be settled. They're always at it,
those Contretemps sneer at each other, priorities
compete. The children stamp their feet
say the Contretemps are stupid
and annoying, they shout shut up!

Sincerely

Television's popular Doctor Psychopath
let loose on the world. What can save us?
The mandala that spins behind the eyes
while you proceed calmly?
The venomous balms the cobra gives
when smeared burn a tattoo
the goddess' shoulder:
eight dragons snarl
breathe fire at the world.

You stir but the knee and paw
are injured, your demeanour,
doh! denouement, make the chase difficult
breathe hard, enjoy the melee
minor deities and maniacs prefer, 'venery',

hunting deer, chasing a girl or burning the Earth.
Creepy, as the officer in charge said,
middle age these days is so T.S.Eliot
(like politicians obsessed with Hamlet's
undergraduate joke solutions).

Bullet-proof, Detective Pharmacy
keeps writing. Tiberius Edifice won't go away
Fidelity keeps the dream frequent,
Sincerely, Kylie Pocahontas.

Legend of the Feral Cat (Bush Ballad)

Big moon glow stencils trees, the
distant screech of a Cuckoo Shrike,

near the creek the ancient enemy is near.
Smell of Rats is in the air.

On waking, Feral Cat kills ten Lizards just to be cruel
and eats Brown Snakes for breakfast gruel.

Wallabies and Koalas have no chance—
are lost when they fall to a cat's voodoo glance.

Flocks of Galahs and Cockatoos fly down moggy's throat
and then she brings up a Billy Goat.

Yellow Dog Dingo put up a magnificent fight
but kitten power won the night.

Slaughters a dozen Wombats for fun
and ten foot Goanna is under the gun.

Tasmanian Devils fade away & Kangaroos
asphyxiate sniffing cat spray. Like old Cicada

shells the Insect Kingdom starts to crumble
pastures fret and forests tumble.

Sheep and Horses lie down. Cattle deplete,
Old man Emu's on the run, Salt-water Crocodiles retreat

to a life deep in the ocean,
a hapless Wedgetail is plucked from the sky.

The thirsty cat drinks the dams and rivers dry,
sandy beaches are for her 'business'.

At sunrise the feral cat moves on
nothing is left by the time she's done.

Spiral

Waiting for aloha hello or goodbye forever,
the earth shifts for a jukebox number,
instrumental, 'Love For Sale', cool and hot,
wordless, each note suggests a word
that can be felt, seen, synaesthesia
jazz always sounds and feels great:
a lingering trumpet turns a mobile phone
speaker into a singing bird, the stereo
grows an extra dimension
to give the brushes and snares space
trumpet echo liberates a room
home of the mind pure and pure:
inspires a joyous spiral
fleet heart and sometimes
sleep rises from the dreadful century
walkin' blissful on a sunny day
blows stars from a trumpet.
Ah, be gone funny valentine saxophone
saved in a bag's groove
floated high the Earth got hot
hot ghosts are still alive, December freezing
3.15 am 1953 too long ago
the blue trumpet notes pop in the sky,
hard buildings, slow cars (some blow a horn)
air pressure drop beginning to snow.
Snowing snow and piano phoenix New York City
tinkling beauty beyond respectable—
sidewalks twist and bend into wander,
oak and maple leaves trodden flat under the black ice,
H being Himself on his tenor sax rescued,
and Herself sings blues, a city weeps.
Together they hit up joy and start to die.

Soldiers (the Sword)

Sunsets, Dad and I walked the dog around the block
and he told me all about his journeys, the places
he'd been in his life. The twenties and thirties were great
until the Depression even then you got by, tough times all right.
Then there was the war when the world turned to shit.
Your war memories amazed me most, kitted out in jungle green
how tough you had to be, diving off a sinking troopship
when it hit a mine, sleeping with your rifle
strapped to a tall tree above the Borneo forest canopy.
The glory of war: weeks behind enemy lines without shower
or latrine, the food tasted like murder and the morphine
wasn't strong enough when they got the shrapnel
out of your back. There was that one time you were shaving
outside the tent, about 5 am before the day's heat and mugginess settled.
Reflected in the tin shaving mirror you see a glint of metal
in the bush that shouldn't be there, the flash from a sword,
katana, or whatever they call it (you almost laughed the words)
you kept shaving and watched in the mirror
the Japanese soldier moving quickly, silently towards you
all you're armed with is a cut throat razor—it'll have to do—
he creeps up and as he draws the sword from its hilt you spun around.
Stunned and terrified the bastard cried *mama*—one fluid
movement like a flattened forehand tore the soldier's larynx out
as he fell he looked into your eyes, he was just a boy
maybe seventeen or eighteen, did not have a blessed hope.
Afterwards you carried the sword in your kitbag.
The jungle heat was powerful, kind of life-affirming
in spite of the killing and the malaria would stay in you
and keep these days to relive in future fever dreams, and sweat
turned your bed into a swamp. You shouted and swore in English
and Japanese the fury of killing and living
it was like being back there with you in that godawful war

as we cooled our dad's burning head with damp towels.
Waking you'd stare and cry for the poor Japanese soldier
and his mama. The sword lay on the wardrobe floor
next to a laundry basket.

Parallel World 101: Hero Product

It was the day after tomorrow the collapse began, the structures
Built and evolved over aeons faded and the striving died, replaced by
Grey resignation and regret that spans the globe.

Tea Time Eat a nourishing meal (legumes and nuts) enjoy a precious
cup of tea, douse the cardboard burning in the fireplace, peer through
the blinds, to see what's left of the world and its stupid glory, charred
and poisoned, still burning in places. The days grow hotter and the air
feels like a dead weight. A few stray drones spy on us. Inside the walled
estates life is almost how it used to be, hydroponic fruit and vegetables
to eat – no meat – running water and electricity twelve hours most
days, gadgets and things often work. The world is calm with less of
us and the cars gone. **Biology** The ocean boiled, its myriads died,
except for sea jellies that multiplied, fused and grew until the ocean
was occupied by a vast coelenterate. Fire, guns and missiles had no
effect, the jelly swallowed ships and submarines, whipped aircraft from
the sky. Chemical and nuclear weapons stimulated, seemed to make
it stronger. Now the Jelly clogs the rivers, blue and white tentacles
spread inland. Everywhere, the drinking water tastes briny. Jellyfish
spawn in puddles and drains, air-borne spores float in the wind, embed
in the skin. The itch is strangely enjoyable, and jellies grow in the gut
and swim through our blood. It's symbiotic—you get used to it. We've
yet to see what comes next, will the tiny jellies fuse inside us? a new
evolution? how human will it be? Forests and wild animals survive in
books, memory and wildlife documentaries. **The Philosophy of Being
Eaten** After the sea-rise, the panic and flight from the coasts, exhausted
people gave up fighting and looting, without treaty or edict decided
to make do, sharing was easier than fighting over what was left. New
theories and cults emerged. Some predicted the rain must stop soon and
the end of the world will be beautiful weather (as Nature or Heaven
intended) and Aliens and/or Deity would attend, or preside, the
cloudless, sunny days then come forever. Others see a new beginning in

the Jelly, the birth of singularity that will swallow life's diversity and survive as a giant monad. Nonsense can make sense, any ideas with an air of consistency will do to explain what's happening. Public debate is an open field of discussion where empiricism jostles with fanaticism, fantasy and resignation. Why or how would Science save us when it gave us the means to destroy everything? It is too late to terraform the Earth. **Excursion** Took the family on the train south, hiked the rest of the way to the coast to see the Jelly and feel its complexity, wide and profound as the poisoned sea that rose and died, a creeping beauty, wild organism that swallowed the oceans. No crashing waves, a giant wobbling freak god, translucent and full of movement and light. You see and think you see things swirl in the jelly, a drowned city's ruins, skeletons, swimming ghosts, and electric arcs sparking from a local nucleus. Children see what children see: *I saw fish in there, I can see people, there's a crocodile, a ship, aeroplane*, they call out, pointing, as if they were visiting a circus, watching a movie or reading a book they love. **Next?** Getting older you start to slow and see some day sooner your own end is coming. Our world is going to hell and the Earth is moving on. Desperately homesick for the past, we'll miss the world's good times when there was a future. Sure, as a species we were warlike, tyrants to each other and doom to our fellow creatures, yet invention and aspiration, the endless fascinations we discovered in the Universe, kindness, nobility of spirit, Life's transcendent moments, art, sport and good fun balanced human evil: we wanted to live. That's how I remember it. Now I can't bear to hear the doomsayers' talk nor the crazy prophets' optimism. One side says *Despair* the other tells us to *Rejoice*, they agree we'll all be Jelly soon. **Peace** Many people step on to the Jelly walk across it maybe fifty metres (a dancer or a gymnast might make it farther) then bubble down, slowly dissolve. Some change their minds run back to solid ground, and if they make it, like everyone else, wait for tentacles to reach out to them or the heart to give up when their blood erupts. Finite time and the end in sight, get on with what's left of life, make the finale dignified, celebrate what you've achieved and where you've been, like you would have done in *the good old days*.

Fresh winds blow the toxic clouds and rain away, the sky turns bright metallic blue. Memory. People madly loved then madly missed: it's time for you all to be together. Happy hallucination! The story's end rushes near. Cry human tears, take time to think about the place your shade might haunt and enjoy the end of the world's beautiful weather.

Original River. First Draft –
Attitude: Don Juan in the Shopping Mall

Thee, best beloved! the virgin train await
With songs and festal rites, and joy to rove
Thy blooming wilds among,
And vales and dewy lawns,

With untired feet; and cull thy earliest sweets
To weave fresh garlands for the glowing brow
Of him, the favoured youth
That prompts their whispered sigh.

Unlock thy copious stores; those tender showers
That drop their sweetness on the infant buds,
And silent dews that swell
The milky ear's green stem.

Anna Letitia Barbauld, 'Ode to Spring'

The earth moved under Parramatta Road and
The wind ruffled a bird of paradise's tail feathers.
Angels' wings shaded toxic sky, a sin of traffic
Exhaled gas and hummed white noise
The car had arrived at its godhead climax
The force for life dominance there is no choice
Listen to car engines all night, breathe poison
All day cars up and down stop and start
Steel demons—obnoxious motors screech and blur
Gorge the atmosphere, their fumes perfume love forever.
The endless traffic zoom drowns speech—roadside, even
A dead dog can be sexy, it's so right to be a maniac.
At night the cars keep coming and coming,
The traffic grew logical. History: doomed hands

Reach up from the steering wheel,
Juan left his chariot parked underground
Inside the mall it's safe and warm. Atoms vibrate
Molecules agitate. 'The mall has it all',
Brings bounty to those blessed by the glitter gods
(Slavery's reward). Shopping's all there is to do,
Except for the wilder young people the mall
Management would like to exclude—they hang
Round and try to grow up and keep out of trouble.
Flamenco muzak is ecstasy, escalators
Are heaven's path. You ride a dragon's spine
Upward upward rise through the shiniest place of all time
Shining the way paradise should shine,
And all the factions of fashionable, glowing
Bliss grows in the fresh fruit's heart strawberry
Rockmelon avocado and smoked salmon
For the masses, the fragrant mix of simmering meat,
Baking bread, hairdressers' vinyl incense
Happy aroma of roasting coffee beans and
Chocolate make life smell great, and taste luscious
And all the ice cream, kebabs and hamburgers in the world.
There's gadget apparition digital virtual electronic
Electric, mountains of myrrh, silver appliances
A dream watch waiting for everyone. Come buy, come buy
Screens and glowing signs, sports clothes, shoes, mobile phones,
Cane furniture, health food and all life's accessories
You name it gear flecked by gold, the mall's levels take
Consumers farther from hell—the mall is happy hunting
Chapel of gleam, a farm and village magic well,
Radiant hub and sacred site two-hundred shops sell
What people want or can afford and the mall gives
Warmth and truth to all the lies—music, tinsel
Pet shops, banks, books, a building full of mirrors
Come to save us from the rubble and the tents.

Shamans can fix or find anything the customer needs
—Juan was expert in his fields—
Most houses and flats are furnished
From the mall and whether his place or hers
Or at a mate's everything was warm, gratifying
Juan was home, felt the mall *satisfying*.
Of course they still ennoble the soul but today's
Best loved poems are the ones that can be enjoyed
During the ads on TV, while playing air guitar
Downloading a game or sitting in an RSL drinking.
Thus this poem will leave much to the imagination—
What is given are some illumination and bursts of story
Something extra for resonance maybe some startling imagery
Maybe not; as far as plot and meaning go
Like Byron's *Don Juan*, this baby is an open field
A map with a lot of *terra incognito*.
A *quick epic* or *verse miniseries* that approaches
The lyric in brevity and leaves time for other play activity.
The trouble, today, with Byron's Don Juan diary
Is the verse smoulders but it's hardly fiery
For an audience accustomed to love arts
Rendered graphic and exploding bodies, too subtle
In an age that dispensed with silken sighs or
Gazing eyes like dreamy comet tails, bon mots
And beaux gestes that actually got you into her pants
Those were the days though sometimes wit
Still works and the Media's kept Bodice Ripping alive
See magazines at the checkout are a soft-core poetry:
The models shimmer vinyl bras and jeans unzipped
Reveal lace delicate beyond belief
But you believe because it's easy to
And gossip is where undead Chivalry
Came to rest—soap opera rules east, west—
Wherever romance is pursued Love is the last adventure

The world where adults grow up to be teenagers;
And this poem too, must only hint at the flame
The smoke conceals in a room of words
and chimera... Every epic has a shipwreck
Juan's boat hit a reef in a storm before he was even born—
Juan's grandparents made landfall and found
An island of streets and shopping malls, paradise
Where all comers are welcome and there's
Nothing doing but love and barbecues.
On land Juan kept swimming.
He swam from birth through childhood and school,
All sticky and metaphorical, learned early
Rules are here to teach limits of behaviour and
Prevent those who would distress society
Learned it's good to have a civic outlook,
Good citizens keep out of trouble and in their own ways
Help progress progress but with migrations
Come the loss of the old verities: beliefs, social bonds,
Family structures, tradition trampled to dust,
And so many brought memories of diverse terrors
Somewhere along the line in a homeland
Turned nasty, sectarian, a world of cruel relativity
But in the land of shopping malls the most fluid entity of all is morality
And this can be delicious so into chaos
Don Juan was born a happy mongrel
(Family background tick multicultural)
Two centuries after the first boat people washed ashore
(With his birth certificate Juan got a medal).
Brought up by MTV in gangsta lore
And rap (read baseball cap) he grew up
During the second New York War
He could be Doan Huan of Da Nang descent,
Or Mohammed Hatim a wayward son of the Mujahedeen
Mario Lanza with a genetic fetish for soccer

Jim Giakos a long way from home in Kiama—or
Any of a million characters—you choose one
Or make a combination and don't give it another thought—
We'll call him Juan. Who cares? whatever.
His forebears came by boat from West, East & North
All shipwreck survivors safely tucked
In bed ashore the island of shopping malls—
Now these migrants call Fortress Australia home
Who wants to be a millionaire? Juan knew
He was a work of fiction working his way to the top
In a zone of esoteric entertainment. Trapped
In a story for Heaven's sake!—a poem reincarnated!
When the good luck gods play a joke—Prithee—life
Should be entertaining. His accent was dinkum
Aussie but to many Juan was dark like a foreign country.
Not everywhere's a mall, outside there's a world
Incredibly sad—huge swathes of continents
Where children search for shrapnel to sell for scrap
Where there's no food on the table, where there's no table
The nearest shopping mall's a thousand miles away—
Light years. Now Juan works the mall like
A missionary or whore searching for a pulse, gazing
At blue windows when security stop and ask him where he's going
Where he's been—times like this he feels too bent
Wished he'd been more like his studious friends—
Doctors, lawyers, bakers, electricians, salespeople,
One was like a tweedy sheik teaching in university
All of them were good citizens populating in new suburbs,
And interstate. Marvellous dynasties.
'Hey Juan!' someone calls from a shopfront.
'Hey Juan your life sucks.'
Life might suck but Juan had a date with Lee Lin.
But that was later, much later at the football club
And there was the matter of meeting Lee Lin's brothers.

We next meet Juan on his way home from the mall
A moment when he's fallen from the mall's good grace
Taken by a near haiku, *Cabramatta Headline*:
Race relations success
these three Vietnamese boys
hit up with skinheads
Nike power can't protect from the demons who
Consume first chance they get—Juan knows he should
Have stayed in the games arcade then gone straight home
Or to a friend's place.
Poetry can be happy therapy hence poetry
In motion—the poetics of space or sport—
Love poems & songs—confessionals and odes to trees—
Performances of mad passion any transcendence
Will do—TRANSCEND—eternal lost cause
And hope of the world—the hope to escape the chains
Of bad faith so often failed—eternity yet
In perspective, back on the pavement, on the road
A car park shows eternity's incarnation—driving in
Driving out—perfect transience flows through the streets
Cries from the babes in prams, the teenagers
Hanging round sing ever onward comes the grave—
Humanity squeezes through the mall like a production line
Up and down the silver escalators
And Juan nodded to acquaintances.
He acknowledged the girls he'd meet later
At pubs and clubs the night time's happy hunting
Where sex's grace linked the freedom in sex's
Echo with the music of talk and traffic
(every five seconds people think about sex).
Juan's lovers came and went, they knew in a world
Growing up, old and dying Juan was okay to spend time
With because pillow talk means you're not dead yet.
Thus sometimes it's good to be desperate:

As with melancholy you don't need to be
Starving to do desperate. Lord Byron the romantic
Saint was wealthy, melancholy *and* desperate
To finish *Don Juan* as the poet knew he'd terminate
Before completing his epic about a man who
Liked to, well, charm houses full of women whose names
Aurora, Julia or Adeline were the many names of roses.
And on a hot night, Juan was cool as.
Some push their luck: the young punk Juan caught
Sipping eagerly at love's chalice—made Botticelli's babes
Express delight—o veiled breasts o comet eyes—
Like its protagonist *Don Juan* was a poem you ought
To go to bed with day after night though ennui might
Lead to putting the book aside, what do you do
When a poem's abandoned or a book read?
Like gone love you think about it and start another.
Don't mention any *isms* or speak morality
Your government drowns refugees, it's way better
At Kandy's flat where her underwear glows and signals:
The angel is coming. Juan swoons, melts and
Swears his love undying. A good time had by all
An eight day romp is a journey like any journey a *trip*
Upon which a youth might embark in the third
Flush of hormones, and writing verse can be
A kind of whipping. The original
Don Juan was composed in *ottava rima,*
A stanza of eight lines of heroic verse, rhyming
Ababcc, it survives here as a kind of primer
On which to paint the words, painting a wall.
History growls in its cage—enough of this gentle
Reader stuff forget the paint, forget the primer it's time to
Log on to level fourteen of the game—a
PlayStation game that has Juan racing street to street
Talking behind hands while waiting in the car

(If he passes through a twirling screen icon
He earns extra life and wins the beautiful princess kung-fu bride).
Juan drives his noble steed *Impreza* gallops hip hop
Through the traffic with six thumping speakers
In the doors & a 24 valve injected motor
Powers alloy wheels—the engine's got grunt.
Floats like a discotheque along Canterbury Road
Finds a place at the bar, the darkness punctuated
By spinning stars—every time he steps out
Of the bar he steps into a new car (dream option)
Where a beautiful girl hands him an orgasm
In a tall glass. 'Keep the dream alive,' a talkback host sieg heils
From the car radio and the listeners proceed
To abuse members of Juan's community,
As if there were no decent people—a straight lie—
As if everyone were all like him, Juan, a sleazy, creepy,
Substance-abusing... blah de blah... The talkback people all
Sounded the same, unhappy. He wondered why.
Far sweeter to be a hot blooded wog
Blessed with passion, Juan loved everyone.
And as if the cool stereotype Juan'd become
Was all his doing when he finished school
Juan couldn't find a job so he got into selling
Pace & ease in the shopping malls' dark corners
And in houses (an easy disaster)—it beats washing
Windscreens—or does it?
Around the corner he met Kandy, Karen or Kelly,
Liz, Liz another Liz, Lydia and Lee Lin, Leanne, pierced
And pretty Lola—a preoccupation with the middle
Of the English alphabet seemed predestined at this juncture—
And they dated and explored for a while
Until Phan and Suzie and Su, Vicki and Yolander
On and on, how many letters are there in the world's alphabets?
And he was so happy he couldn't get anything done.

The best place for a bush ballad is the city
A meeting that has created our times' great power myths—
And where love must always go wrong
The urban cowboy, tribal battles, the town mouse
And the country mouse and best of all the sincere
Young Miss who brings humanity to a man's monster soul.
Together they confront life's disasters, she the mistress
He the master (enjoy the luxury of comedy and soap opera)
She didn't save Juan, he found the cliché too corny
But her social work manner made him ultra—.
Juan craved love the way a poem might dream
Many readers or parched travellers chase mirages
Through the desert—Juan found his oases real enough,
Was at one with his calling to see loveliness
Like a bird set free by touch and kiss and
Share his wicked happiness. In uncertain
Times Juan was slippery plain and simple,
But most folks didn't mind—they liked his natural wit
The way they might like a butcher or a therapist.
Juan took care of himself worked out hard
At the fitness centre near the mezzanine.
He danced like a bee with serious sting as tensile as a
Loaded spring a num chukka on a fling he
Was… and he felt psychically good (psychic cheer)
Every five seconds he thought about sex
And Juan's mind made love with the atmosphere,
His gods are fine with most of this,
And in his own way Juan was really a feminist.
Women rule in life, they should run things.
Like lions men should live their natural lazy lives
When Juan was out of it he might philosophise.
A naughty feminist Juan wakes at noon
And hears high heels clatter down the hallway.
Across the suburbs… the escalators call to him,

Driving to the mall he'd seen the troika
Of hairdressers who made New Year's Eve
Such a treat, a shocker. A hard body is always
On vacation but works the overtime. Superficial?
It beats being Hitler or Martin Bryant
Or some bastard profiting from children crying.
Everyone here's happy polluting the world
With their garbage and dreams
And with Nature dying for humanity
Juan knew it was too late to save the Earth, so
He might as well enjoy the technology and the girls.
Too much good time was like swallowing
A karaoke machine all sparks and smoke
The microphone hanging out of his shirt
How many femmes fatales does it take
To change a light bulb? Juan drank and watched
Angels fall through the atrium clasping harps and trumpets—
Their buckets and brooms dropped from heaven on Juan's head—
Juan wrote in his journal next to the evening's meaningless
Drunken scribble: 'consume, be silent, die'.
To pray to Madam Bountiful helps make sense,
—*Give me the universe's love and make me*
Be a great grandfather happy till the end
O ancestors I will not upset tranquillity
& please intercede on my behalf with spirits
Of generosity, good luck charm—please—
Thank the lady for granting wonderful life
Bless all the ancestors who helped build the world.
There are eyes and there are souls
There are classics, romance and adventure
There's the kind of love that's beyond love
There will always be a place for truth and harmony—
Somewhere there are places—of fresh air and clarity—
To go—the way watching a video is easier than reading

Is why Juan didn't need to go to those places,
Except maybe the eyes and soul.
He learned from TV that puddles multiply the moon
And the white moon trapped in quiet lily pond
Distracts lovers—them moaning full deep—yes
And once you had the hearts and eyes
If you're honest
There's no need for sincerity.
Romance, however, is always necessary.
Outside the malls and the clubs there was
No air conditioning and poison clouds gathered.
Juan celebrated his thirtieth birthday—
'Baby,' he said, 'I love this 21st century,
'But all those years wasted.'
There's the matter of Lee Lin's five brothers.
Five Brothers. They gave Juan a choice
A fine brother-in-law, or a sticky ending.
There's nothing like a shotgun
Wedding to focus and give closure.
The old Don Juan's gone, for a while,
Headlong into Lee Lin's Dynasty
And while the world around them
Grew cold and mean
Juan's and Lee Lin's hearts entwined.
A chance… Juan steps up to the next level.
He's pushing a stroller in a shiny new mall
A new vicinity.

Epilogue and then

Depressing hotel nights when the only love
Was on video? Solitude honed the instincts and hunger
Aroused the madness. Love, Television tells us,
Is a daily quest, guides the soul to happiness,
Love fulfilled or tragic, gentle and caring, a journey together.
Profuse metaphors make the love birds sing.
It's an athlete's game. A relationship.
We last met our hero settled down and working every day—

A libertine's purgatory. But work involved travel.
After a week of lonely hotel rooms (a day for each month of
Marriage), Juan began networking and soon
Had a girl at every retail outlet, picking him up at the airport.
The years passed and all the coming and goings
Grew numberless like the stars. Voices purred,
Warm breezes blew on a river until the airliner
Took off. Life insisted the aim of existence

Was shared abandonment. Blessed by the bikini
Goddess, if heaven is attained by faith or love,
Juan preferred the latter's ritual. Without practising
Love's philosophy, life would be endless
Variations of misery: no one to desire, no magic.
Without lips and breasts to adore, and hot
Words at breakfast time, kisses on the balcony
What would be the use of charm? Still, his mind's

Vampire recesses held a premonition the Universe
Might not reward stray kisses and that night a shadow
Walked through the front door, lights flickered,
The bar-radiator died and Juan's spine rose like a dog's hackles,
He felt fear like a child shouted at by a stranger in the street.

And while the shade made herself at home the house
Chilled ice cold. After giving her a good once-over,
Juan sighed, this angry spirit needs some loving tenderness

(Western and Country) to free her from a frozen realm.
She started dropping in more often. Juan had never gone
Out with a ghost before. Besides, who wouldn't take Death
To dinner? Her ashen lips whispered him into a trance.
Don Juan is such a fool! Luckily, apparitions don't
Expect you to do the deed (at least on the first date).
The vision melted as Juan was slapped awake
When your heart's on fire 'forget everything',

He remembers, 'because she's my heaven…'
Tomorrow was a future spiralling and the past was
Catching up, divorce letters flew back and forth—
Cupid shooting poison arrows. Lately, Juan's been
Trying to give the ghostly girl the slip but she keeps
Appearing in odd places, quiet moments, thoughts and dreams.
Back in the shopping mall, Juan steps onto an escalator
Climbing up, up to the next level and he sees—GAME OVER—

Don Juan Enters The Underworld

… Became unbearable, the road to hell
Aches with good intentions.
The last conscious word is a cheeky whip bird's
Wistful whistle then sucked down
A hole in existence, the guard rail is no obstacle.
At Lover's Leap there was nothing to do but plummet.
Oh, bloody whipbird has the final word
The stones and sticks spin like wheels, no ledge

Juts to break the fall, head first down a scree,
Try grab, but bounce (don't try this at home).
The universe clicks her tongue. 'Hope,'
He'd have cried, if he had any, 'I'll never abandon…'
Branches and rocks tear his flesh as the earth
Parts its lips to allow entry when extra
Dimensions of time and space come into play.
A cheerful mountain devil winks.

What happened? Nightmare waking up
Just in time? This time, a force like a tornado
Holds the body in place until the senses leave
And the soul travels the darkness war and death
Journeyed to get into this world, tough trip
Full of guilt and grief and regret, old archangels
Say some souls profit from the torment.
Don Juan sniffed sulphur in the air

Remembered he'd been here long time ago
Doomed by a statue's curse, on the say-so
And signed statement of the lady's maid
Never a pretty situation, but give him a break
—it was back in the fourteenth century—

And more recently cast in Hell
(If he had nine lives, how many to go?)
Trapped in relentless conversation

With a geriatric superman
And an unlikely crew of others
Compiled by the playwright Clunky Greybones:
A sweaty season of amateur theatre, voices
Projected, the dialogue shouted and furniture
Banged around the stage. Can do,
Those who can do, eternal headache
Too many words, that playwright

Should have stuck to teaching,
Don Juan the much loved poète maudit
Gets a free ticket to the underworld.
He hears the Beelzebub chorus sing
Fling 'em down, toss them in
The bad, hopeless, forlorn, regretful, whatever
Turns on your misery, time to calculate
How many vices equal a sin—o toss 'em in.

A spiral is always down because it makes
A laugh wicked, ah ha ha, to see someone
Ride the slippery slide, and age shall not weary
When it leaves them for dead. Line up, line up
On your Bridge of Sighs. Juan recognised
A beautiful starlet—was she his guide?
Who immediately asked him not to mention
Her when he was out and better.

Trashy magazines sucked her blood, she'd been unwell
Juan said 'I didn't know you'd died.' 'I haven't,
I'm still going through hell' the babe replied,

'You don't have to die to burn here, even the rich
And famous...' she sighed, 'everyone wants a
Piece of you and when they get it, life
Becomes Hell Central, cars chase you to madness
Dammed paparazzi are demon assholes,' she cried.

Juan felt the pop princess's pain and so busy
Was she nurturing it he left her there glowing
With the power of a trinity: I, Myself and Me,
What the world needs: another diverting autobiography.
Juan could dispense with a guide—he'd read the texts.
Clever authors had made the journey, did
Something rash or stupid that tickles Pluto's fancy
Like drunks swimming with a crocodile,

Hearts float in rum and whisky, the higher
Than high space cadets trip the light smashed
Fantastic, an army of manic depressed fabulists
And for the legions suffering writer's block,
Where else is there to go but down into the inferno?
Bravely finished a clutch of sonnets,
The heavy lifting done and nothing left to do
But to open a vortex, say a hit on the head

Or a painful divorce that drives you
Into the arms of the delirium tremens.
A line for the deceased and one
For those souls who prefer a living hell
A shambolic crew lining up with passports,
Curricula vitae, scribbled notes
Old tickets, envelopes or what-have-you.
Don Juan joined the queue.

The poets are well represented.

Some even get a residency
Since so many write so sweetly
Regarding the simply diabolical, the great
Eschatologies are travelogues.
Dante's map was an intimate geography
He populated with his enemies
A bit sinful in presumptuousness, hubris

To second-guess divine intention
(Touch wood) earned him a place
In the Demonic Poets' Hall of Fame.
Besides, Islam's angels would never let him
Enter Paradise. Baudelaire planted flowers
Incubated in the rebel being's brain
That Milton understood too well—
Ah, so many poets of the devil's party

All dust and bones now, gone to hell
Or the other place. But before this discourse
Sinks into a lesson it gathers its wits
And begins to explore. Don Juan
Hears the Beelzebub chorus sing
Sees a herd of words, dark, chattering,
Serifs and antennae twitching like cockroaches
As they watch him walk to the cliff and open a door…

So this is where bushwalking gets you—Devil's Staircase
Or Windy Lookout. The world lost its colours
And became a flat, sepia landscape engraved
In the mid-nineteenth century, the sky
Absolutely starless. Now the herd of words
(lI I Xr hello1.whot fathered the notes
that were or tie herd- div o ID ye of title faith
get lleG thee behind me Satan and the herds

of words rollesmea ??? .milled araound o
their awful 'tentacles and Satan itching
crazy soccer balls an evil rugby called war
destroy destroy hurt your kids
11it should have been me' me the diodes decides decides
r okay oeoypggzi okay zsp ? It was the beginning
of the words hellish words that would come
out an evil mouth or be the germ...)

Had grown, letters bumping each other,
Nudging each other toward him like segments
Of a millipede, the words played scrabble
The leery letters broke away, joining together
With others to form new words.
Suddenly, they were crawling all over him
Like ants, and rhinoceros beetles, scorpions
And spiders, a carnivorous alphabet

Bites and stings, denoting and connoting
Confusing the mind with concentration
When it could be semi-conscious at play
Half in the backyard, half in the lounge
Two places at once. Bad words slip
Into the world hardly visible, at first,
Harmless enough they're only words—
The serifed and sans-serifed bugs

Sounded out hard utterances,
Words planted in young minds to grow,
Anger and kill on children's tongues
So calorie food hilltop antibiotic court-martialled
(Blissfully) at Millrace: Itinerary encounter!
Collateral Damage. Paperboy! Paperboy!
Your call is needed. Civilian Congratulations:

Tom and Mary went down to the dairy,
And so it went, a vulgar delight jackpotting
Every now and then with bull-shaped words,
'Do to Urania', space-cows
Or Ntis the sloganeer, no basis, though
Blissfully (a coat hanger theory)
Now they are many-headed attack-hounds
Leaping mouth to mouth, o they be sea-snakes,
Miss Viola Verse is reading tonight

For one night only, reading from Blackjack and
Poker, games of chance. Is he focus?
Was he essence? Kisses, hugs and roses
Return the soldiers' bones to us.
Ich bin ein clubber. 'Tis radiation
And every bad thought brings an accident.
As for the original Fall, what choice
Were those kids given. Stay dumb

Divine monkeys in a softly softly garden
Or rebel and grow up in a world of woe
Lifetimes and ages to seek some meaning,
Judgement an eternity beyond the pale
Sepulchre, the end of the road, the trail
Comes to a point existence and memory fuse.
Possums laugh, their bushy tails point to the sky.
'Lost Paradise?' they ask. 'Regrets?'

Acknowledgement for poems previously published is made to:

The Age, All Together Now: A Digital Bridge for Auckland and Sydney
(http://www.nzepc.auckland.ac.nz/features/home&away/index.asp),
*Australian Poetry Journal, Best Australian Poems 2014, Big Bridge
(US), Canberra Times, Cordite, Jacket2, Kitaab, Meanjin, Southerly,
Sydney Morning Herald, Tincture.*

'Original River. The First Draft of Attitude: Don Juan in the
Shopping Mall' and 'Don Juan Enters the Underworld' were
published as part of a *Rare Object* chapbook, *Don Juan Variations*,
published by Vagabond Press, Sydney in 2012.

Lightning Source UK Ltd.
Milton Keynes UK
UKHW040725110220
358531UK00001B/83